*F*orever is the only language our love speaks, and you are the love of my life.

— Donna Fargo

*This book is dedicated to everyone who believes
in the unlimited power and beauty of love.
It's for those who embrace love as the greatest gift
we are given and the one true miracle that can unlock
the secrets of the soul, set us free from all fear, overcome
the toughest challenges, and heal the deepest hurts.*

*These words are for all those who desire to join with
another person in allowing love to teach them,
humble them, and perfect them together.
It's for those who want to experience the glory of life
and the meaning of true love with someone who inspires
their hopes and dreams, shares their successes and
failures, and loves them no matter what. It's for
anyone who believes that love is the reason
we are not meant to live life alone.*

To the Love of My Life

A Collection of Love Poems

Donna Fargo

Blue Mountain Press ™
SPS Studios, Inc., Boulder, Colorado

SPS Studios, Inc.

P.O. Box 4549, Boulder, Colorado 80306

Contents

You Are the Love of My Life

Deep within my soul, where my secrets are kept from even me, sometimes I feel feelings that I cannot describe. They're sacred and they're private, and they're all about you and me. They tell our beautiful love story, for you are the love of my life.

Our hearts speak an "eternal" language of undying devotion and loyalty. No one can ever know this place with me, and I will never find this place with anyone else but you. We are soul mates, lovers, and friends. Forever is the language of our love, and this is our love story...

You show me you love me by your commitment to me. Your actions speak the truth. Your expressions tell me your feelings. You define your love for me by the way you treat me. Our love is not a place we came to and left. We stayed. It is not something that will go out of style or change in time. We have a sacred trust. You are the love of my life, the one in whom all my dreams and hopes and plans are committed.

In our secret place, our private world, we talk about things no one else will ever hear. We forgive each other when we break promises, and we start over again. We're on each other's side, and that's where we'll always be. We don't undermine our relationship by talking about each other, and we don't betray each other's confidence. Time has taught us some things well.

I am thankful for this blessed relationship. We are together in every way. Our love is not something we feel just today or just for the moment. We will not exchange one another for anyone else. I have faith in our love. Our love doesn't have a timeline. It not only shares todays and tomorrows but creates destinies. Forever is the only language our love speaks, and you are the love of my life.

With All My Heart, I Want to Thank You

For those times I've missed saying
    "Thank you,"
I want to thank you now for being
    a soft and gentle light in my life.
Thank you for the thoughtful things you do
    for me... not out of obligation,
but out of the goodness of your heart
and in the spirit of love and concern for
    my happiness and well-being.
You bring so much joy to my life,
and I want you to know that I appreciate
    everything you do for me.

Thank you for the loyalty and trust you inspire.
Thank you for the lessons in humanity that
    I have learned from you.
Thank you for being such a beautiful example
    of a caring person.
I know I've said it before, but it is worthy
    of repetition...
I love you and I appreciate you,
and I want to thank you for
    everything you do for me.

I Love You for All
That You Are to Me

You're my partner in every detail of my life. Although we don't always think alike, we take responsibility for our decisions and actions together. You want the best for us, and your actions bear out that desire. You think of things I wouldn't, and I respect your judgment. You ask my opinion and try to please me while making your suggestions, too, and I depend on you probably more than you could imagine.

You're my best friend. Besides wanting the best for us, you've shown me time and time again that you want the best for me. You want me to be happy and you always have my best interest in mind. You know my weaknesses, and you try to protect me from my own problems. When I have feelings I need to process about others and about ourselves, you help me to be more objective. You often have much more balance than I do, and you always add a unique perspective that I might not have considered because I'm too close to the situation. I can discuss anything with you.

We trust each other implicitly. Our private concerns are sacred to us and don't often need discussing because each of us knows how the other feels. You're understanding of my fears and funny ways, and you even appreciate some characteristics of mine that I view as personal faults. We laugh together and cry together. We've been through valleys together and touched mountaintops, and we've grown closer through our experiences and circumstances.

You're the love of my life. I wouldn't want anyone but you. I am committed to you forever. You have shown me time and time again how important I am to you. Thank you for honoring my dreams and helping them to come true. You're more than I could have asked for, and I feel blessed that we have each other to love. I'm so thankful to be sharing life with you. You make me feel special in so many ways, and I love you for all that you are to me.

Every Day,
I Say a Prayer for You

*E*very day, I pray for you, give thanks for your life, wish you the best, ask the heavens to bless you with good health and happiness. I surround you with thoughts of hope and faith and love. I ask your guardian angels to protect you and keep you safe from any harm and to blanket you with joy and contentment and peace and prosperity.

I ask that you be guided with the wisdom to make choices to enhance your life and the awareness to make changes that are in your best interest. I wish for you a storehouse of opportunities, the ability to meet your goals, and the joy of your own approval and acceptance. I wish for you your heart's desire, every need met, every prayer answered, and every dream come true

Every day, I say a prayer for you. I ask that you be prepared for whatever life hands you or whatever you're going through. I ask that your spirit be strong and lead you and guide you each step of the way down every path you take. I ask the universe to confirm for you that you're someone very special. I ask the earth to be good to you, and I ask God to show you His perfect way.

No Matter What I Say or Do, I Love You

I know we have our unhappy moments... when things aren't going great or we hurt each other's feelings or we say things in the heat of an argument or we do things we wish we hadn't. But after the storm is over, after we try to see each other's side, after we calm down and put things in proper perspective, after we apologize and ask each other's forgiveness... we realize that we're just not perfect, all our rough edges are not smoothed out yet, and we don't show our love perfectly... and then we forgive each other and go on.

As much as I try to change my ways, become more mature in my thinking, learn patience, slow down enough to listen and be objective and not take things so personally, I still fail at times and say or do something that almost upsets the foundation of our love. I just want you to know that I am always sorry for that.

I also hope you realize that those hasty words and careless acts are not indicative of my true feelings. They are just fleeting, momentary displeasures. They are unprocessed emotions, my immaturity speaking, my unguarded reactions. They are not the whole picture, but rather just a little blot on the corner of the canvas of our relationship.

The truth is... I love you all the time, even when things aren't perfect. I say things that hurt sometimes because I'm hurt. I sometimes do things without thinking of your feelings, and at times I just do things without thinking of the consequences of my own actions. Please understand that I never mean to hurt you. I think sometimes part of the problem is that men and women just react differently to situations and see things at times only from their own perspective. Please forgive me when I'm not sensitive to your needs and feelings.

I'm not perfect, and I don't want you to think that I'm making excuses for my behavior when my actions seem insensitive and unloving. I will continue to work on trying to show my love to you in a more caring way so there is never any doubt in your heart and mind that I love you and I will always love you... no matter what I say or how I act.

I Think We're Blessed

Although things aren't always perfect between us, and certainly not always easy, as I look around us, I think we're blessed.

Some people don't have someone special in their lives, like you and I do. They don't have someone to share their joy, their problems, their solutions. They have no one to learn life's lessons with and to help them grow stronger. They don't have someone to tell things to or to forgive them if they mess up.

Some people don't have an everyday companion to be there for them in every bend in the road. They don't have someone to worry about them when something in their life is going wrong. They may not have anyone to pray for their safety and well-being and happiness.

As I think about what could and could not be, I'm thankful for what is and what isn't. I'm thankful for you, for me, for our love. I'm thankful for what we do have. I'm thankful that we have each other, and I hope you are, too.

I think we're blessed.

I Used to Dream of Falling in Love with Someone like You

I used to long to have someone I could talk to about anything; someone who would know my heart and good intentions and love me in spite of my imperfections; someone who would respect my feelings, however weird they might seem, and forgive me when I made mistakes.

I used to dream of finding someone who would see past my faults and unprocessed emotions that cause me to show sides of myself that aren't finished developing yet and may never be, someone who would love me in spite of them and yet be able to see the love in my heart, no matter what tried to cover it up.

I used to hope that someday I'd find someone who'd accept all of me and who could appreciate the attributes I bring to a relationship, too. I wasn't looking for someone who was perfect. I was just looking for someone to love and be loved by, someone I could share my most secret secrets with, someone I could trust forever. Well, I found that person in you.

We've been through the rain and the fire together. We've survived some ups and downs that could have caused us to go our separate ways. I just wanted you to know that I appreciate you, I thank you for being you, and I'm so thankful we are together.

I realize now that my dream has come true. In you, I've found that someone that I can share everything with... the good, the bad, and all the in-betweens; the hard times, easy times, the messy and the clean. We've been together through it all, and I just want you to know that I think you're pretty special and I am lucky to have you. Please keep on being you and loving me. I love you so.

The Moment I Met You...

Before I found you, I thought I knew what it was like to be in love, but really I just knew how it felt to be in "like," because...

Everything changed the moment we met and your heart collided with mine. Like a flash, I was swept into an awareness that I had been saved for you, for true love.

At that moment, there was no other question in my mind except... when would you and I begin spending the rest of our lives together?

And I have never regretted my decision.

I Found My Perfect Love
When I Found You

You're the best there is, and you make me want to be the best that I can be for you. You inspire me to want to do all I can to make you happy and proud of what I do. We have fun together. You encourage me rather than discourage me. You are patient and understanding. You've been good for me and to me in every way. We balance each other with our differences.

You complete me and make me happy to be alive. You're thoughtful and considerate. You turn my heart into a sacred place where our love lives and grows stronger every day, safe from the humdrum of life, a place that no thief could steal and no amount of upset could move.

I appreciate your unconditional love more than it is possible for me to express. You accept me no matter what. You overlook my shortcomings, forgive my mistakes, and love me anyway. You don't hold grudges, and your ability to forgive easily moves us beyond our hurts into understanding and maturity.

You are my friend, my partner, my love, and I'm so lucky that you are sharing your life with me. Please remember that no matter what happens during the ups and downs of our relationship, the moments will be very few that I won't just be loving you with every fiber of my being and wanting you to be the happiest person alive. I hope you know that my love is forever and you are my perfect love.

You're My Best Buddy
in the Whole Wide World

Sometimes I wonder what I would do if I didn't have you to talk to, to listen to, to be myself with, to ask your opinion when I need another point of view, and to help me do something I need to get done. I guess I'd be talking to myself a lot because I can't imagine anyone taking your place. It really means a lot to me that you're always there for me, and I feel so lucky to be in love with someone who is also my best buddy in the whole wide world.

It's a good feeling to know you're not just there for me in the fair weather but in the bad, too... you're not afraid to get wet with me in the storms and down and dirty with me when I need a cleaning partner... you don't mind helping me with the boring stuff when two heads are better than one. We've been through a lot of changes together, and I guess that's why you are so special to me.

I love you for a lot of reasons. You're easy to be around. You give me my space but let me know you're there if I need you. In this fast-paced, impersonal, and sometimes unfriendly world, I know I'm really fortunate to have someone in my life who is so loyal, dependable, and trustworthy, someone who is also... my very best buddy in the whole wide world.

When We're Apart, I Really Miss You

*P*eople talk to me, but I don't hear them. Their words float in the air until my mind finally acknowledges that I need to give some kind of response. My daydreams aren't even dreaming. I feel bored, lost, uninterested in much of anything. I pick up the phone to call you, but it's the wrong time or I know you're out of reach. I really miss you.

There's no one else I want to talk to about whatever is happening or not happening in my life. I go through the motions and do all the things I usually do, but my heart knows I'm not my usual self.

My life is on hold. I look at the clock and the calendar, and the hours and the days take on a renewed sense of length. Time stands still. The nights take forever. My sleep is restless. My life is on "Pause... waiting." I just really miss you.

I pray that you're safe from all harm and you're feeling all right, that you're healthy and sleeping well. I miss your laughter. I miss our talks. Sometimes I almost cry and say it's for no reason, but my heart knows better. I'm just sad, and I really miss you.

I'd Be Lost Without You

My fondest hope is that you want to celebrate every day with me, seize every moment to enjoy our life together, and experience every second of our love as a rare and precious gift. My secret wish is that you want our love to last forever and that we will be together always.

What I love most about my life is living it with you. I am so thankful to know the kind of love we share. You make me so happy. You bring me joy. I feel so fortunate to know that dreams do come true and love is a trusted force that directs our hearts to know what is best for us.

In the deepest part of my being, I know that I'd be lost without you. Our dreams and goals keep me hoping, caring, and planning. Because of you, I wake up every day excited about life. Our love is the reason I have a song in my heart. I want to go on sharing my life with you forever and I hope you will celebrate every day with me, my love.

These Are My
Special Wishes for You

I wish you love in your life, hope in your heart, faith in your dreams, and encouragement enough to do whatever would make you happy, keep you healthy, and assure you the prosperity you deserve.

I wish you joy. I wish you peace. I wish you blessings in your life. I wish you answers to all your questions, resolve to change something that you want to change and the awareness and ability to accept something that perhaps you haven't been able to change.

I wish you satisfaction in your work and all the other things that would make your day-to-day life more balanced and content and rewarding. I wish you the capacity and knowledge to embrace the gift of love that dwells in your heart and is replenished when given away.

Everyone is unique and different. I hope you can appreciate your own uniqueness and realize that you're an angel in disguise to some, a friend so important to others, and a member of a family with whom you have significance and importance beyond description.

Special people change our lives, make us feel better about ourselves, and help us to realize our dreams. They give us a sense of community and belonging. They make us feel appreciated and accepted and move us toward our own emotional security.

Because you're so special to me and to everyone else who loves you, I wish for you your heart's desire. May God bless you and keep you always safe and sound.

You're My Favorite Person in the World

I am blessed with the greatest blessing one can have: to love someone with all my heart who also loves me. Because of the gift of your love, you mean everything to me.

You make my world all that it is, a much better place than it would be without you. I can't even imagine what it would be like if we weren't together. Our love defines my life, and it is what I'm most thankful for.

You're the one I want to spend every moment with: every dream, every wonder, and every goal. You're the reason that I care about trying to do anything, the one I want to please besides myself; you're the one who knows every corner of my soul. You're the one I love enough to give my life for, the one I want to breathe my last breath with; you're the biggest deal of all. If there's one thing I know, it's this: You mean everything to me... I love you... and you're my favorite person in the world.

There's No One for Me but You

Whether I'm looking at the
    shadows of the clouds on the
    green rolling hills
Or seeing the shadows of my doubts
    about something I did or said,
It's a pure and simple blessing
    to have you in my world and to
    share everything in life with you.
You light me up. You help me through.
When I look back and wonder
    about the ones I didn't choose,
I'm glad because I know that...
There's no one for me but you.

You're my partner; you're my friend;
    you're the love of my life.
You're the answer to my questions;
    you're the dream that came true.
It's a pure and simple feeling — I love
    someone with all my heart — and
    that someone loves me, too.

And no matter where we go, no matter
  what we do,
You are my life. You are my world.
You are everything to me...
There's just no one for me but you.

Whether the terrain in life is rocky
  or the ride is fairly smooth
Or the goals are stubbornly
  refusing to be reached,
It's a pure and simple fact that
  it's okay if I don't win some
  game — I've got all that I need
Because you've got me, and I've
  got you
And that's all that matters, all
  that counts.
I love the one I'm with...
And there's no one for me but you.

You're My Guardian Angel

You settle me down when I struggle for balance; when I try too hard, you remind me to get out of my own way.

You let me learn my own lessons; you're my guardian angel, taking time out to dream with me and time out to play.

When I'm all out of confidence and down to my last hope, you help me restore my faith in myself.

I've learned from you never to give up, that this, too, shall pass, and there's nothing to fear but fear itself.

You've taught me that nothing is impossible if we just believe and where there's a will, there's a way.

When I've lost my direction, thanks for being my guardian angel and for helping me find answers to the prayers that I pray.

Thanks for giving me a reason to trust, someone to care about, and a blessing to be thankful for.

Thanks for speaking a language that my heart understands, for carrying me on your wings and helping my spirit soar.

When there are no formulas to follow and no map for where I'm going, thanks for helping me believe I'll find a way.

Thanks for being real to me, my guardian angel, not just someone I made up to help me feel that who I am is okay.

When Life Hurts Me the Most, You're Always There

You provide me with a shoulder
   when you know I need to cry.
You're happy for me when I need
   someone to share my joy.
You listen to me when I need to talk,
   and you talk when I need to listen.
And when life hurts me the most,
   you're always there.

You're with me when I make mountains
   out of molehills.
You know my weak spots better than anyone,
   and you also know my strengths.
You share my dreams. You know my faults.
   And you know most of my fears.
And when life hurts me the most,
   you're always there.

You know what makes me happy, and
you know what makes me sad.
You've seen me make mistakes, and
you've seen me beg forgiveness.
You've seen life treat me right, and
you've seen life treat me wrong.
And when life hurts me the most,
you're always there.

I'll Always Be Here for You

I know I may not always say
    the right thing at just the
    right time,
And as hard as I try to do
    things that are best for us,
    I sometimes make mistakes.
I don't want to change you...
    I love you just the way
    you are...
And I hope you know that no matter
    what life has in store for us,
    I'll always be here for you.

We've grown closer through the years
and I believe the future will only get
better for us.
You mean more to me than anything
or anyone else in the world.
I always try to put you first because I
want to do everything I know to
protect our relationship.
I don't want you ever to have a doubt
that I'll love you forever, and I'll
always be here for you.

I try to be the kind of friend you
need and the best partner to you
that I can be.
I really want to learn from our
mistakes and do my part to keep
our house a home.
I'm committed to our relationship, and
I vow to do all I know how to do
to make our dreams come true...
I love you with all my heart, and
I'll always be here for you.

My Love for You
Comes with a Lifetime Guarantee

My love won't cost you a penny. It is given to you without a price. The warranty requires only one condition for lifetime service: that your commitment be a choice made freely and maintained faithfully.

This guarantee insures that the facts are as stated in the contract we made when I said I would "love, honor, and cherish you — for better or for worse, for richer or for poorer, in sickness and in health, and for as long as we both shall live." Very simply put... my love for you comes with a lifetime guarantee.

Although it's possible that it may appear bent and strained at times from the wear and tear of life, this love is very resilient, given a reasonable degree of patience and time. It is forgiving always and can be made even stronger with dreams shared and promises kept.

I hope you will enjoy this love, appreciate its infinite reliability, trust in its sacred features, value this perpetual friendship, and rest in the fact that it comes with a lifetime guarantee: never to grow old and only to get better in time.

I'm So Glad I Get to Share This Life with You

Let's go out and touch the sky today. Let's marvel at God's awesome creation: the cotton clouds, the sunshiny day, the life-giving air, and the fruitful land. Let's lie down in the green grass and roll over and over. Let's blend ourselves into the landscape and rejoice that we're alive. Let's get close enough to a bluebird that we can almost touch its feathers, but let's be really quiet so maybe we can sit and watch it and it won't fly away. Let's play in a field of daisies, pick some wild flowers, and give someone who's not expecting it a bouquet. Let's sing in the sunshine and walk with the world, release all our cares into the atmosphere where they can't weigh us down... and then let's just watch them disappear.

Let's be accepting of ourselves and each other and feel the freedom to be just who we are, the way we are, unique and different, not wrong or right, not worthy or unworthy, not weird or perfect, but okay. Let's just let ourselves be happy and satisfied, lacking nothing, but appreciating each breath, each picture, each feeling, each thought, every memory, and every sigh.

Let's claim this day as our special gift from God. Let's find a pretty tree and use it as a chapel to pray... "Thank you, God, that we're alive and have each other to love."

I'll Always Believe in You

...and I Know You Can Make Your Dreams Come True

I am confident that you can do anything you set your mind to. Whatever hopes you have for your future, I believe you can find a way to make your dreams come true.

Whatever challenges you face in life, I believe you'll turn every experience into something positive. When you have serious questions you need to answer or emotions you need to process, I know that you'll take your time and do the right thing.

Even though there may be times when you'll be dissatisfied with the way things are going in your life, I know you'll learn the lessons you need to learn and eventually make the changes you need to make and move on.

I want you to know that I am always thinking of you, praying for you, and wishing you the best. If you need me to talk to about your concerns, I'm here to support you, just like I know you are for me if I need you.

Besides being the most important person in my life, you are a very special and wonderful human being, and I'll always believe in you.

I Wouldn't Share My Heart
with Anyone but You

You're the love of my life, the one I choose to dream my dreams with. You're the one I want to be with to make memories I can keep. You're my soul mate in the morning and the evening of my life, the one I sleep beside in my bed. I'm committed to our future and our present and our past. I'm devoted and dedicated to you, and fidelity is not something about which I am likely to change my point of view. Loyalty is the virtue that I treasure most, and to me the heart is sacred ground. I would share my words, my efforts, some of my feelings and my secrets, but I wouldn't share my heart with anyone but you.

I Give You My Word

I promise to love, cherish, and honor you all the days of my life. I'll be with you through eternity or for as long as you want me. It is my most fervent wish to be the kind of partner you desire.

I pledge to stay with you through whatever challenges we have to face: poverty or wealth, sickness or health... anything.

I want us to be together always... to share every triumph, every joy, every disappointment, every experience. I want us to celebrate every breath of life together.

I promise to be faithful to you. I will always keep our vows. They are sacred to me. I am committed to you for life, no matter what we have to deal with. I don't want anyone else but you. You are the love of my life.

I promise to protect our devotion to each other. I will do everything I know to do to nurture our love and relationship and give you all the love I am capable of giving. I want to be your best friend as well as your sweetheart, now and always.

I promise to try every way I know to keep our love alive and well and thriving and always new. I promise to listen when you want to talk, to forgive when you need forgiveness, and to do my best to understand when you need understanding.

I promise to stay with you forever and love you with all my heart. I give you my word and seal it with a prayer and a kiss.

A Love Note from My Heart to Yours

If you could open my heart's door and step inside, you'd be overtaken by an atmosphere of love that would take your breath away. You would feel arms so loving, a heart so caring, and feelings so strong that you would lose all track of time. You would be transported by a power so extraordinary that nothing would be impossible for you. You'd float on cotton candy clouds that would make you smile. You'd lose every care, every pain, every burden. No fear could live in this presence. Every anxiety would melt away... And you'd know that you had inspired all this love.

There would be a light so warm and real that it would lift you and heal you of any hurt you've ever experienced. It would take away every worry in your life, and erase even the slightest scar on your soul. You'd know the essence of a magical love that paves the way for memories and smiles too sweet to capture in word pictures.

I love you beyond any expression that I could come up with, but I hope you can feel the enormity of emotion and overwhelming joy in my heart because I'm so in love with you.

I Love You with All My Heart and Soul

These aren't just some more simple words, more recycled thoughts to take up space. They're not one more excuse to find a way to pass my time. These feelings were born in my heart where my love for you resides, outside the confines of my mind. They matter to me because I'm sharing them with you. If I leave out something, I hope you can read between the lines and feel the feelings I am trying to convey. It's important to me that you know without a doubt that... I love you with all my heart and soul.

These words may not seem sacred to someone who has never loved someone and been blessed with that person's love in return. They may just seem like more words that have been said before, so they're nothing new. They may seem wasted and unreal to someone who isn't in love with someone like you.

But since these words are the tender expressions of my love for you, they become my gift to you. So... for lack of fancier words to convey my feelings... I love you with all my heart and soul.

It may sound like I'm trying to indulge your fantasy or boost your ego, but I don't want anything except for you to understand that these words are all I have, besides my actions, to show you my love. And because they are the truth from my heart, I hope they mean something to you. I love you more than I guess I will ever know how to tell you. I just hope you can feel the feelings these words wish to convey. I've said them before, and I'll say them again... I love you with all my heart and soul.

I Will Always Want You with Me

I will always want you with me,
    no matter where life leads,
To share with me all the dreams I dream
    and all my hopes and needs.
Whether I'm sorting through my cluttered
    thoughts or climbing some familiar wall,
I hope you're there with me every single
    winter, summer, spring, and fall.

When things are going right and when things
    are going wrong,
When life throws me a curve, when I'm weak,
    and when I'm strong,
If I had a million wishes and they could all
    come true,
I would always want you with me...
    they would mean nothing without you.

We've shared the good times and the bad...
    we've been up and we've been down.
We've been bound by our own chains, been
    the fool, and played the clown.
But we've stayed the course together,
    and by your side is where I'll stay.
I will always want you with me, no matter what
    and all the way.

Let's Remember
These Ten Golden Rules
for Staying Happy with Each Other

1. First and foremost, let's realize how lucky we are to be in love with each other. Let's say "I love you" often with gifts of praise to show our love. Let's remember that love grows in an atmosphere of freedom and trust, not from restraint and obligation. Let's do things to keep our love and romance new and alive and never take love for granted.

2. Let's listen objectively to each other, as we would to a friend, and remember that acceptance is a key to understanding and a buffer for tension and resentment. Let's not take things so personally but give each other the right to have different opinions, the right to disagree.

3. Let's never stop treating each other like sweethearts. Let's talk to each other as sweethearts and do things that sweethearts do, like… share the chores around the house and work together in achieving our goals. Let's do things just to make each other feel loved, especially when we might be feeling a little down. Let's take pride in the way we look and act, but never let external values have more importance than the internal feelings of the heart.

4. Let's always take care of each other, go to the doctor with each other, put the other one first, but don't neglect our own needs either.

5. Let's talk about things together the way we would talk with a friend. Let's absolutely refuse to say anything negative about each other. Let's keep our own identities, but walk together as one and never give up on our love.

6. Let's settle the fact that we've made our choice and we're no longer looking for anyone else.

7. Let's be in agreement about how our money is spent. Let's be sure that big items should have the approval of both.

8. When in doubt about our actions, let's ask ourselves how we would want to be treated and then act accordingly. If we've argued, let's never go to sleep without asking the other's forgiveness, even when we don't feel like it or want to. Let's do what will make us both the happiest in the long run and be the best for our relationship.

9. Let's remember that we're in this life together and never let our problems or concerns get out of hand and make us go in opposite directions. Let's be joyful that we've each made a commitment to the other... through sickness or health, poverty or wealth, or whatever comes along.

10. And let's have fun... always!

You Are the One
True Love of My Life

True love is the bond that won't be broken
  no matter what the challenge.
It's the bridge to our future and the door
  from our past.
It's togetherness, when separation could
  always be an option.
It's never giving up on each other
  and the love we want to last.

True love is a commitment to keep our
    promises; it's staying together because we
    want to.
It's the ultimate satisfaction; it's the soul's
    celestial gate.
Sometimes it doesn't make much sense
    and it plays by its own rules,
But the heart is homesick without it
    and it's well worth the wait.

When the world's rules are changing,
    true love will hold fast.
It won't take for granted, and it won't
    change with the tide.
It won't be discarded like some out-of-style
    fashion.
It's the real thing, not something counterfeit
    just along for the ride.

True love is something very special...
    it's forever and always.
I may sound old-fashioned,
    but I don't care if I do.
Ours is no ordinary love,
    and if no other dreams come true...
I know I've found the one true love of my life
    and I'll never stop loving you.

About the Author

*With her first album, **The Happiest Girl in the Whole U.S.A.**, which achieved platinum album status and earned her a Grammy, Donna Fargo established herself as an award-winning singer, songwriter, and performer. Her credits include seven Academy of Country Music Association awards, five Billboard awards, fifteen Broadcast Music Incorporated (BMI) writing awards, and two National Association of Recording Merchandisers awards for bestselling artists. She has been honored by the Country Music Association, the National Academy of Recording Arts and Sciences, and the Music Operators of America, and she was the first inductee into the North America Country Music Associations International Hall of Fame. As a writer, her most coveted awards, in addition to the Robert J. Burton Award that she won for "Most Performed Song of the Year," are her Million-Airs Awards, presented to writers of songs that achieve the blockbuster status of 1,000,000 or more performances. Donna continues to tour extensively throughout the United States and other countries.*

*Prior to achieving superstardom and becoming one of the most prolific songwriters in Nashville, Donna was a high school English teacher. It is her love of the English language and her desire to communicate sincere and honest emotions that compelled Donna to try her hand at writing something other than song lyrics. Following the success of her first book, **Trust in Yourself**, Donna has chosen, with this new title, to share some of her deepest and most intimate thoughts on relationships... and the love of her life.*